The Butchery

BASTIEN VIVÈS

FANTAGRAPHICS BOOKS, INC.
7563 Lake City Way NE
Seattle, WA 98115
(800) 657-1100

www.fantagraphics.com

Follow us on Twitter and Instagram
@fantagraphics and on Facebook
at Facebook.com/Fantagraphics.

TRANSLATOR: Jenna Allen
EDITOR: Kristy Valenti
SUPERVISING EDITOR: Gary Groth
DESIGNER: Chelsea Wirtz
PRODUCTION: Paul Baresh and Christina Hwang
ASSOCIATE PUBLISHER: Eric Reynolds
PUBLISHER: Gary Groth
PUBLICITY: Jacq Cohen

ISBN: 978-1-68396-447-6
LIBRARY OF CONGRESS CONTROL NUMBER:
2020950080
FIRST EDITION: 2021
PRINTED IN China

THE BUTCHERY

Bastien Vivès

Translated by Jenna Allen

CLACK!

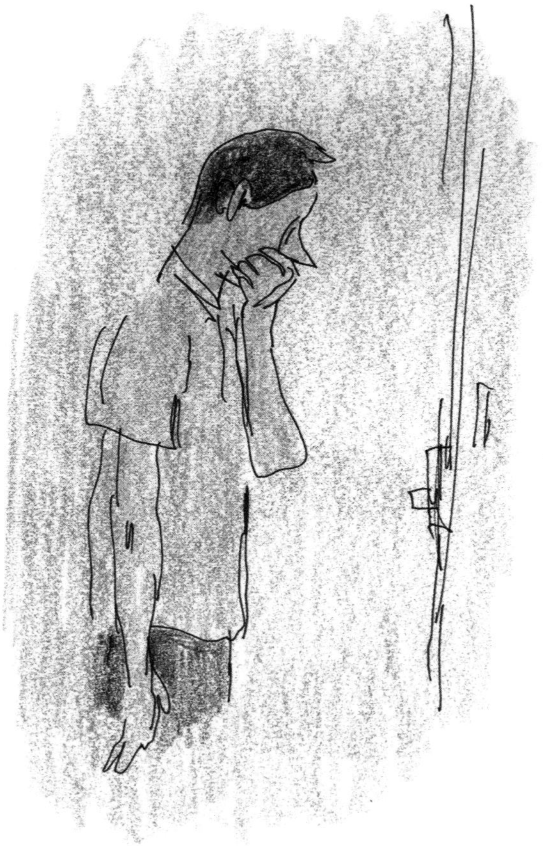

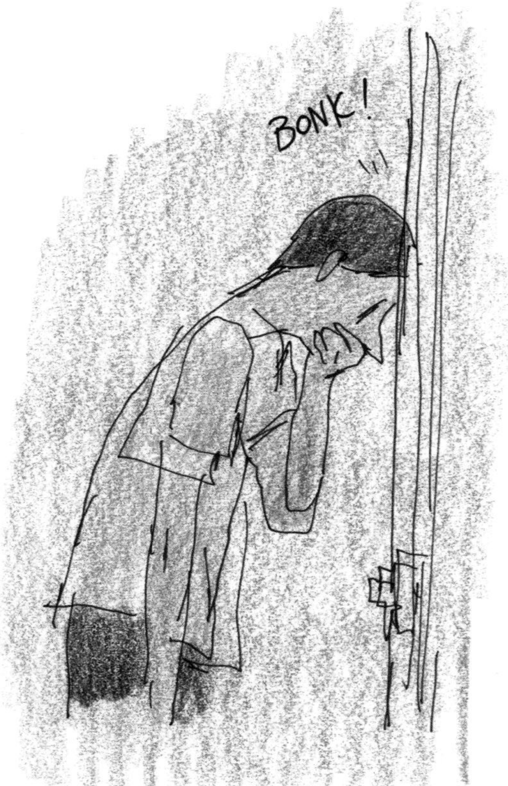
BONK!

RiiiiiiiNG !!!

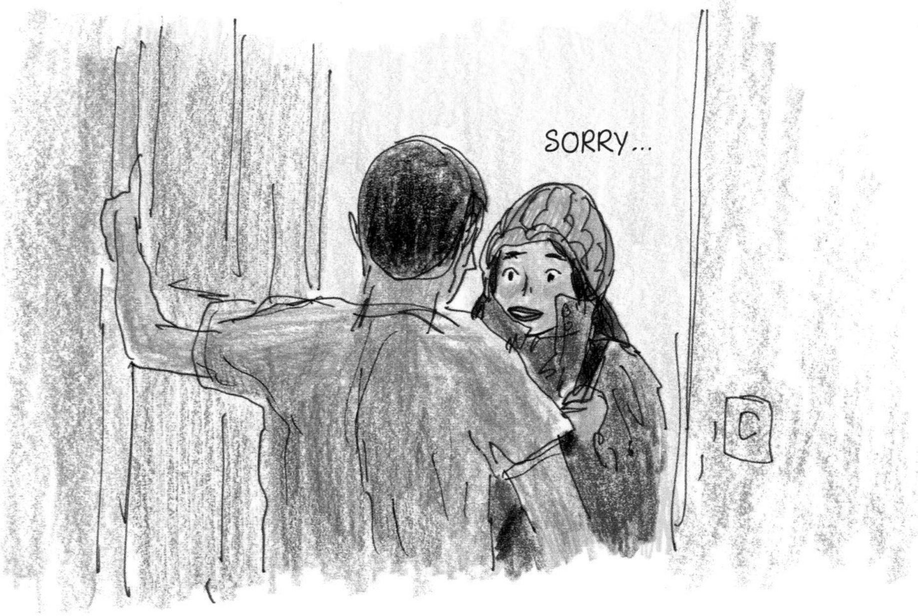
SORRY...

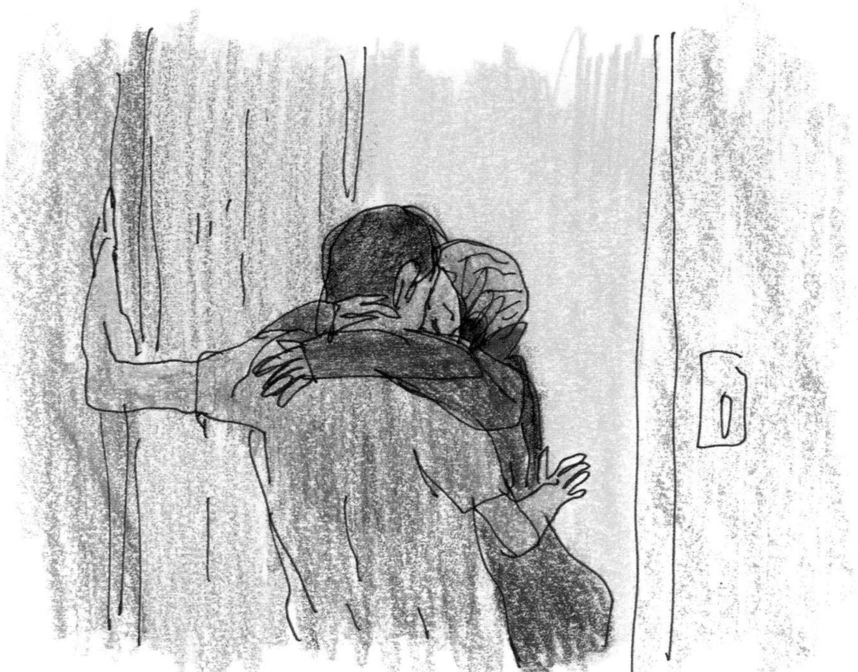

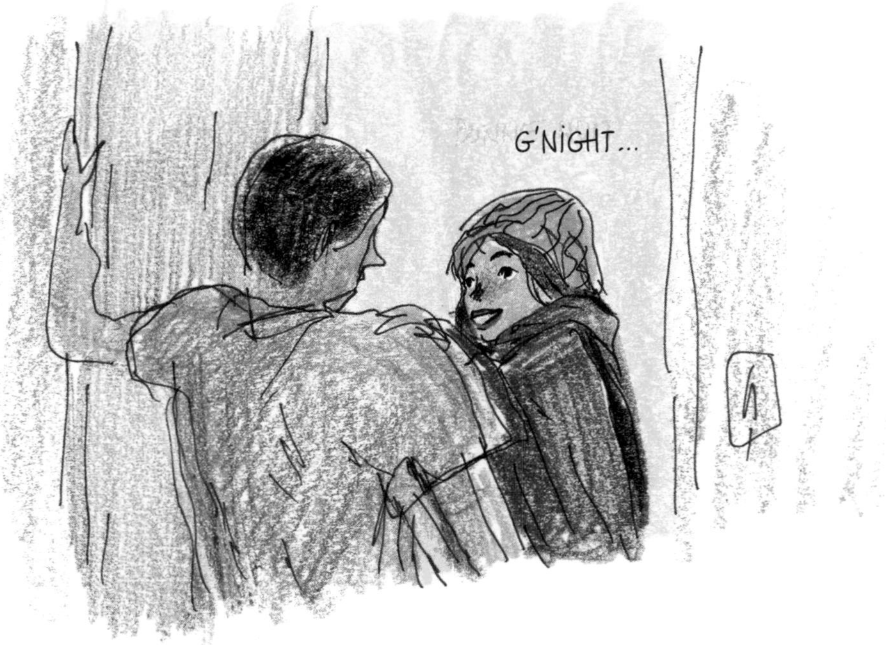
G'NIGHT...

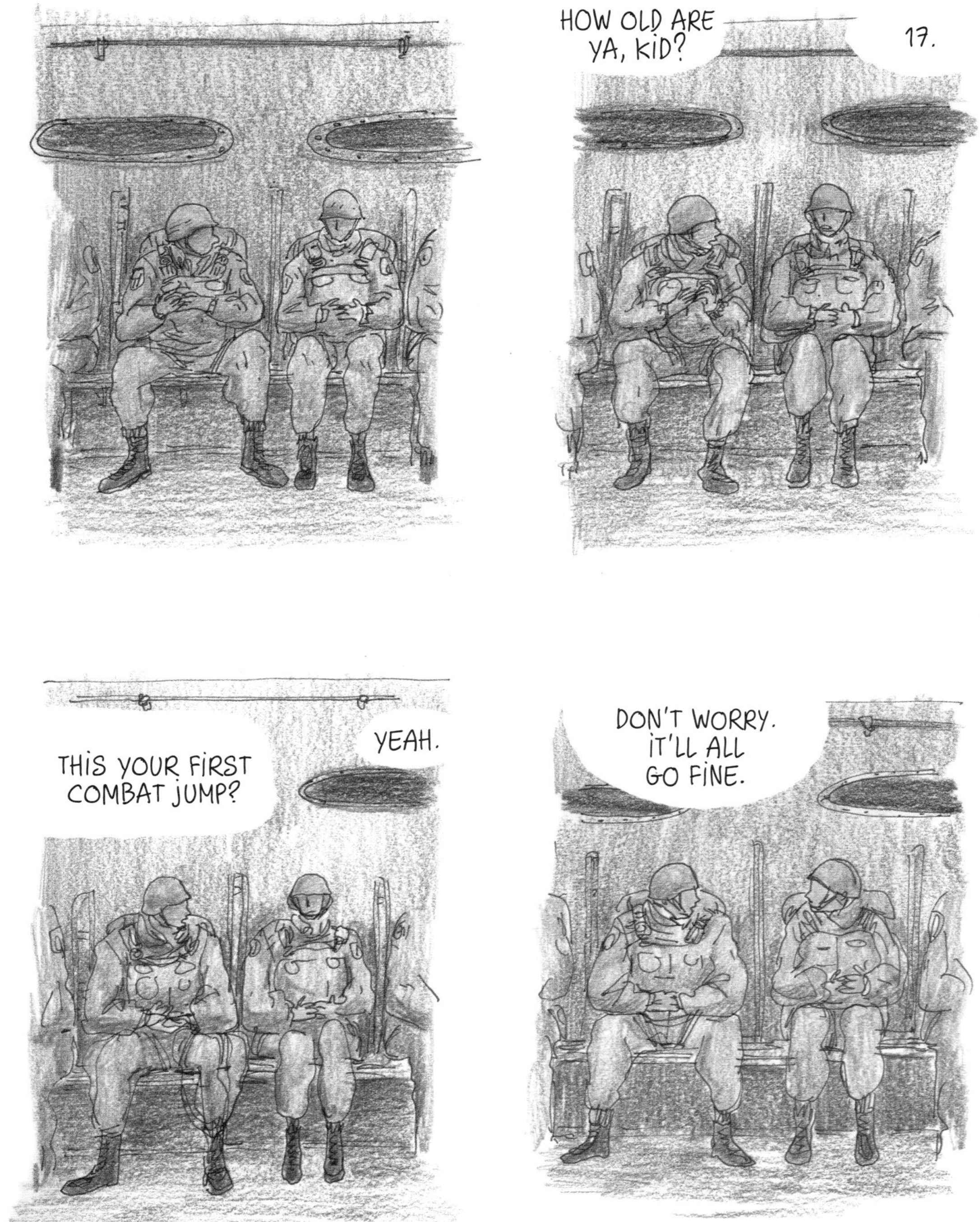
HOW OLD ARE YA, KID?
17.
THIS YOUR FIRST COMBAT JUMP?
YEAH.
DON'T WORRY. IT'LL ALL GO FINE.

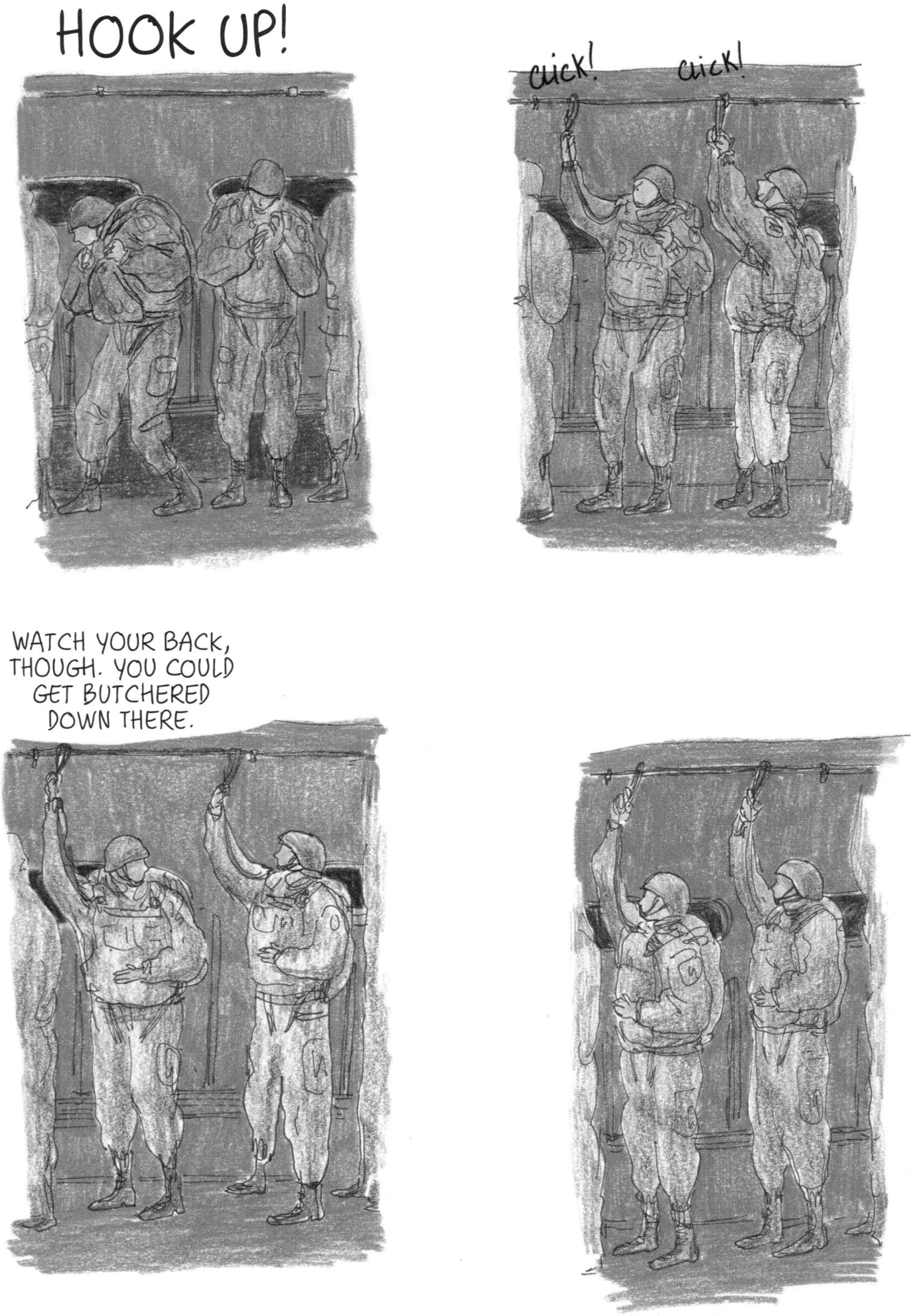
HOOK UP!
CLICK! CLICK!
WATCH YOUR BACK, THOUGH. YOU COULD GET BUTCHERED DOWN THERE.

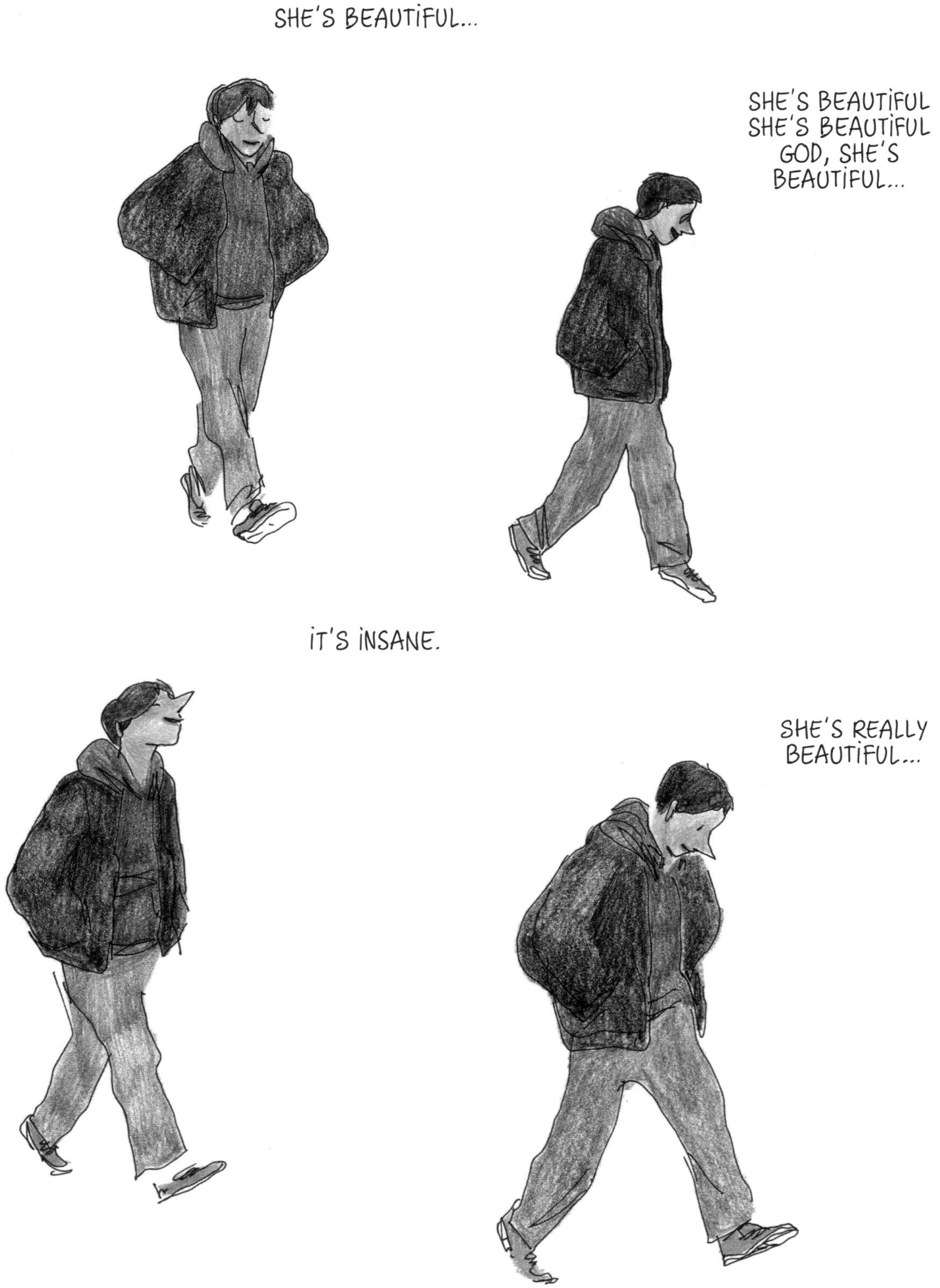
SHE'S BEAUTIFUL...
SHE'S BEAUTIFUL SHE'S BEAUTIFUL GOD, SHE'S BEAUTIFUL...
IT'S INSANE.
SHE'S REALLY BEAUTIFUL...

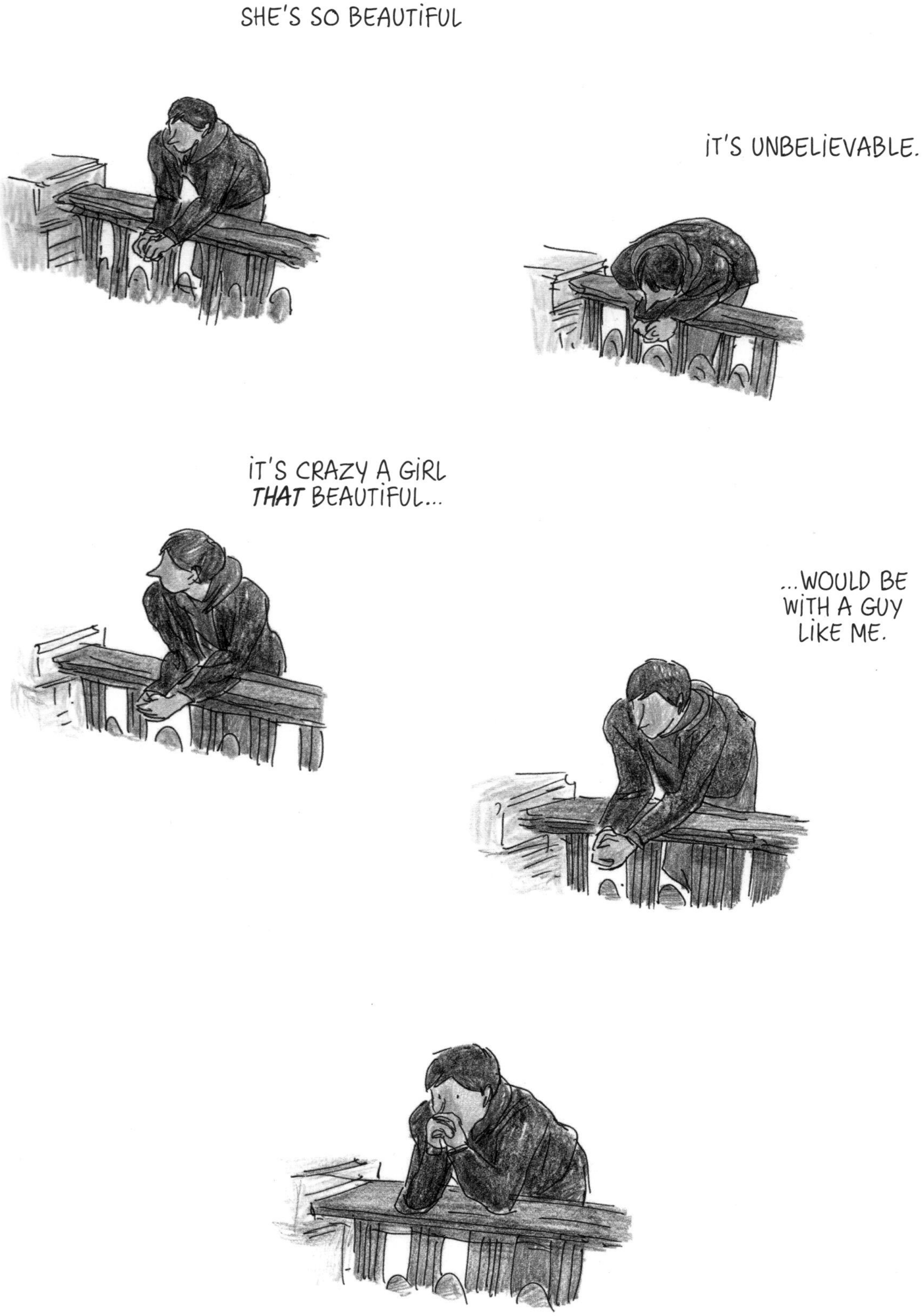
SHE'S SO BEAUTIFUL
IT'S UNBELIEVABLE.
IT'S CRAZY A GIRL *THAT* BEAUTIFUL...
...WOULD BE WITH A GUY LIKE ME.

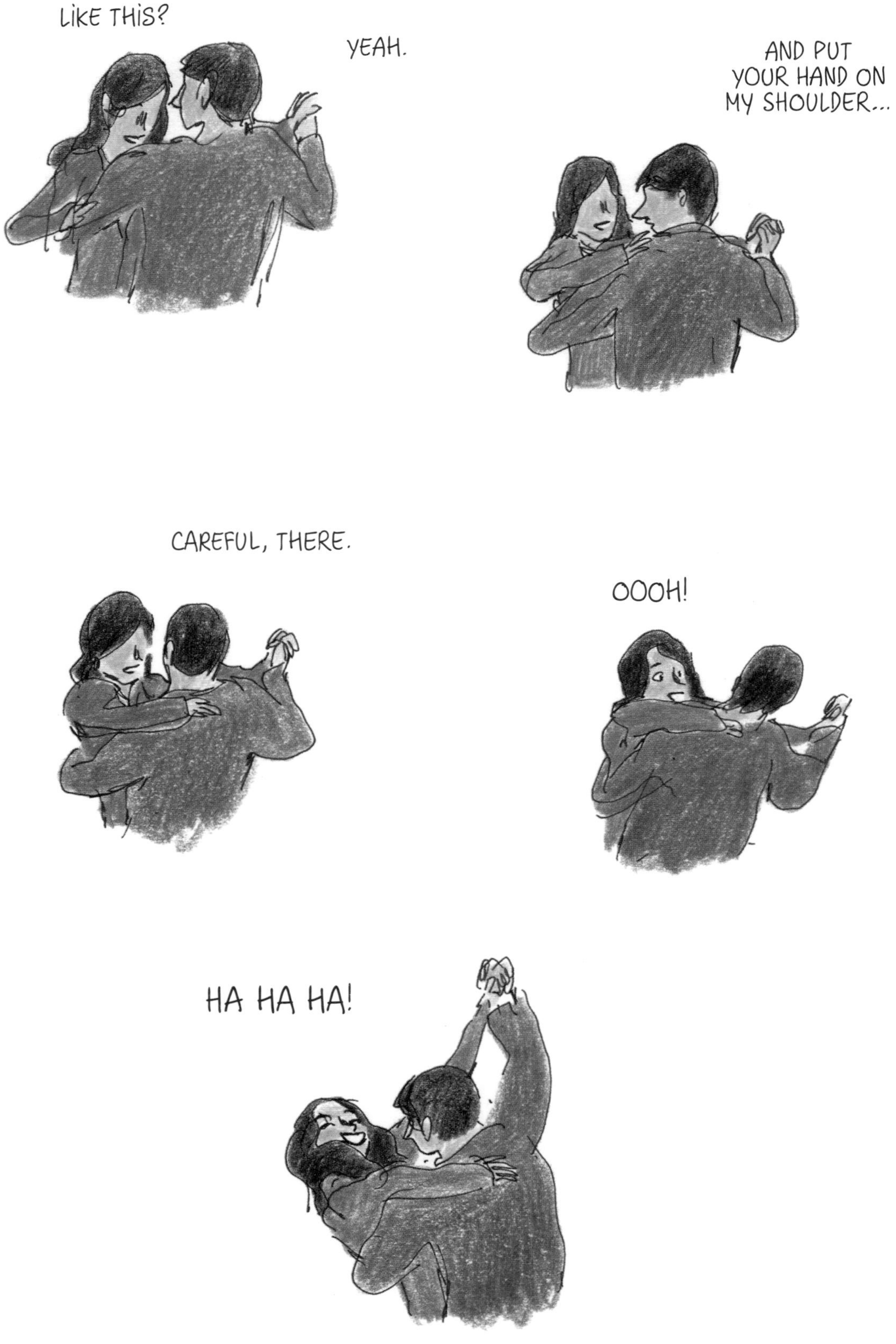
LIKE THIS?
YEAH.
AND PUT YOUR HAND ON MY SHOULDER...
CAREFUL, THERE.
OOOH!
HA HA HA!

YOU CAN'T
ACTUALLY
WALTZ, CAN
YOU?

NO, REALLY, i CAN.
i'M A PRO.

JUST WATCH,
HA HA.

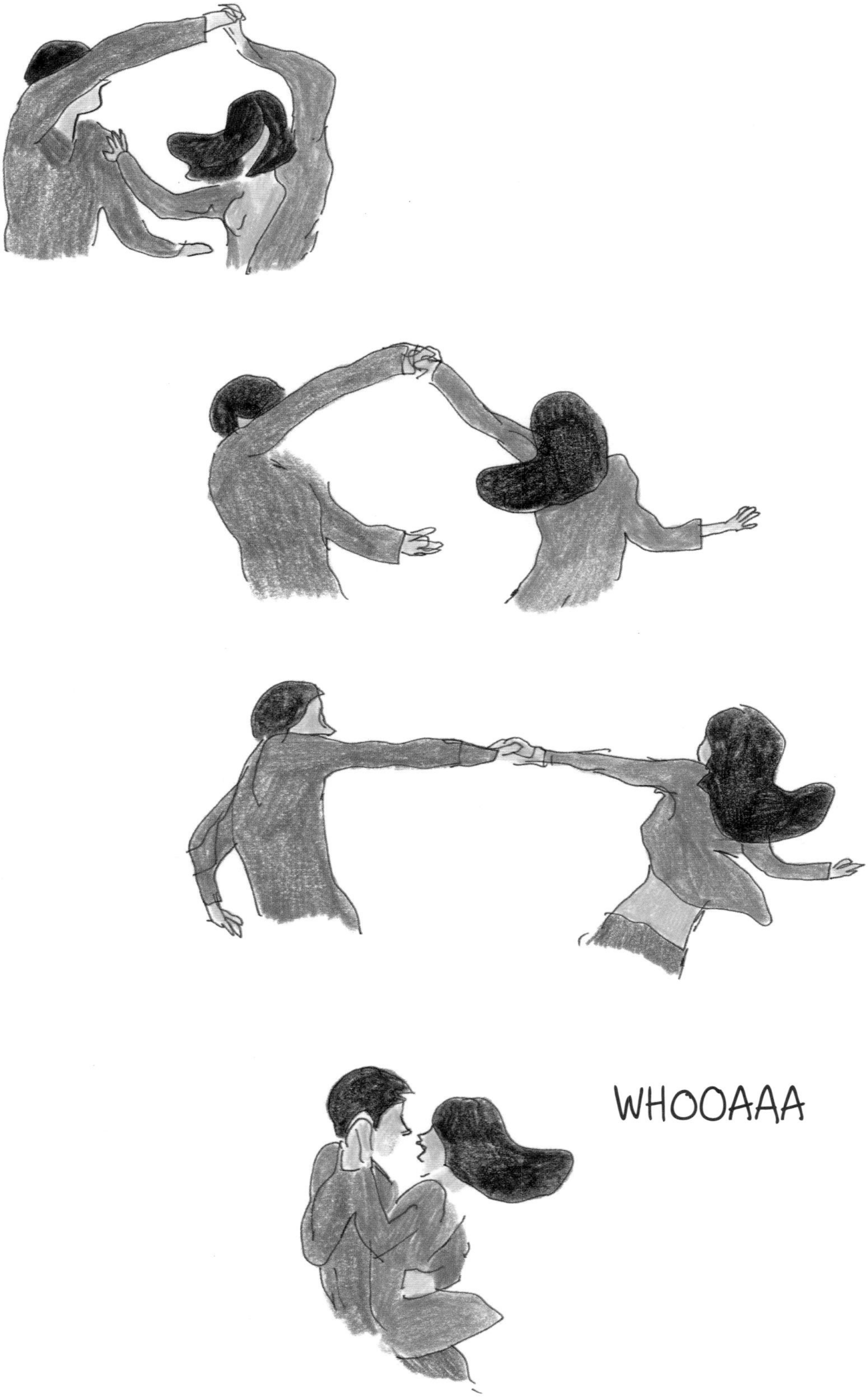
WHOOAAA

KEEP UP!
iT'S GETTING
FASTER!

...TA-DA!

WHEE!

HA HA!

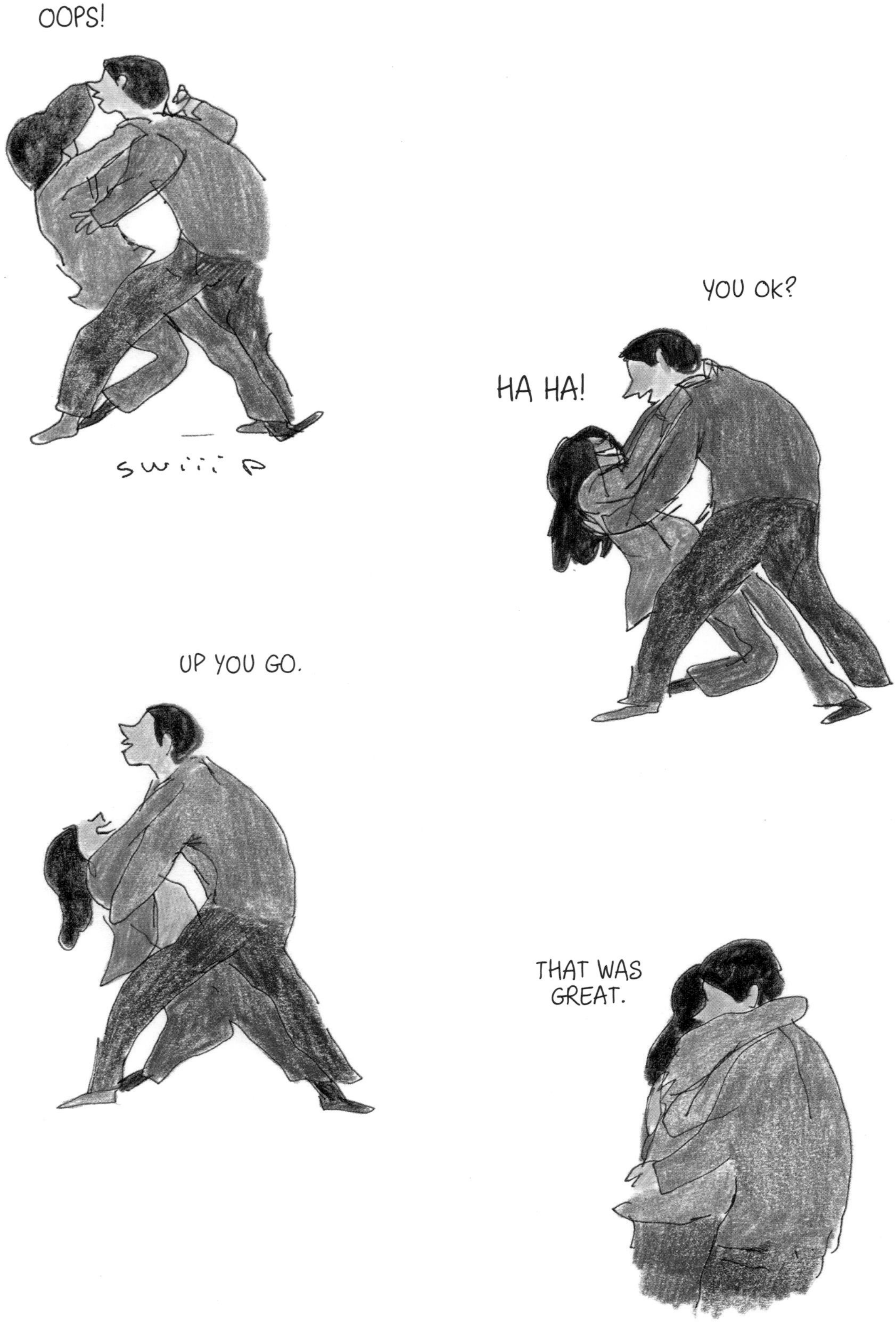
OOPS!
swiiip
YOU OK?
HA HA!
UP YOU GO.
THAT WAS GREAT.

HOLD ON!

i'LL PLAY iT AGAIN.

YOU FEEL LiKE
GOING TO THE
MOViES?

WHY NOT...

OR WE COULD GO
FOR A WALK...

WHERE D'YOU
WANNA GO?

I DUNNO.

OR WE COULD GET
SOME GROCERIES.
THERE'S NOTHING
TO EAT.

MMMMM...

WORST CASE,
WE COULD
EAT OUT.

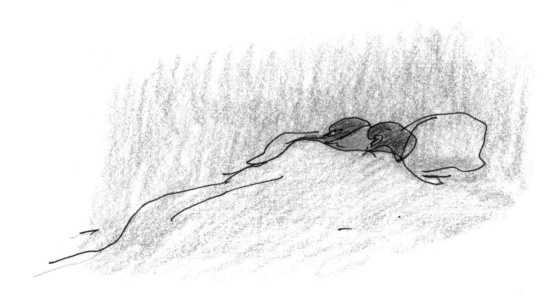

CLICK!

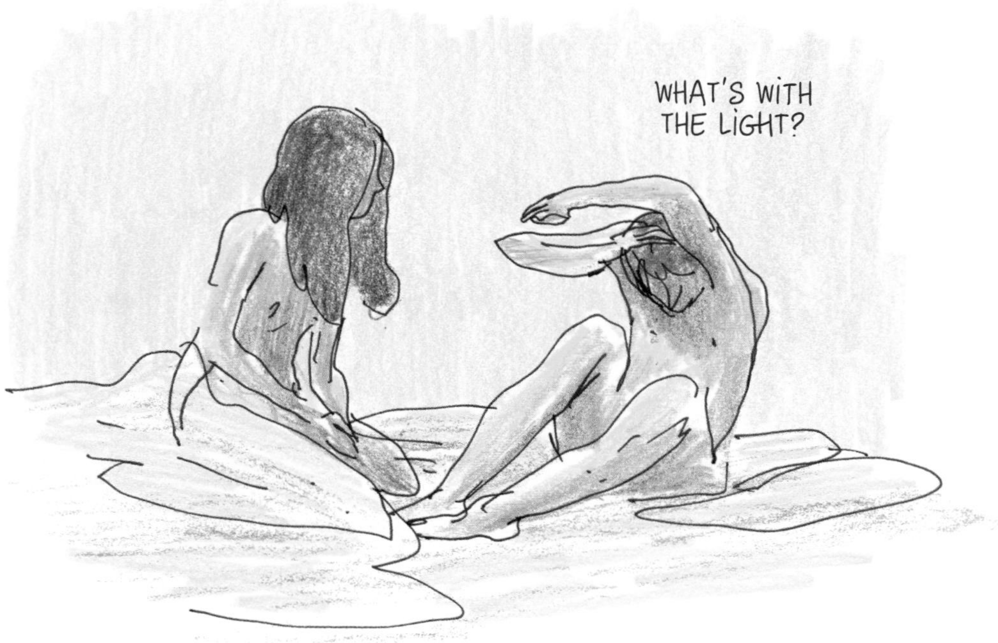
WHAT'S WITH
THE LIGHT?

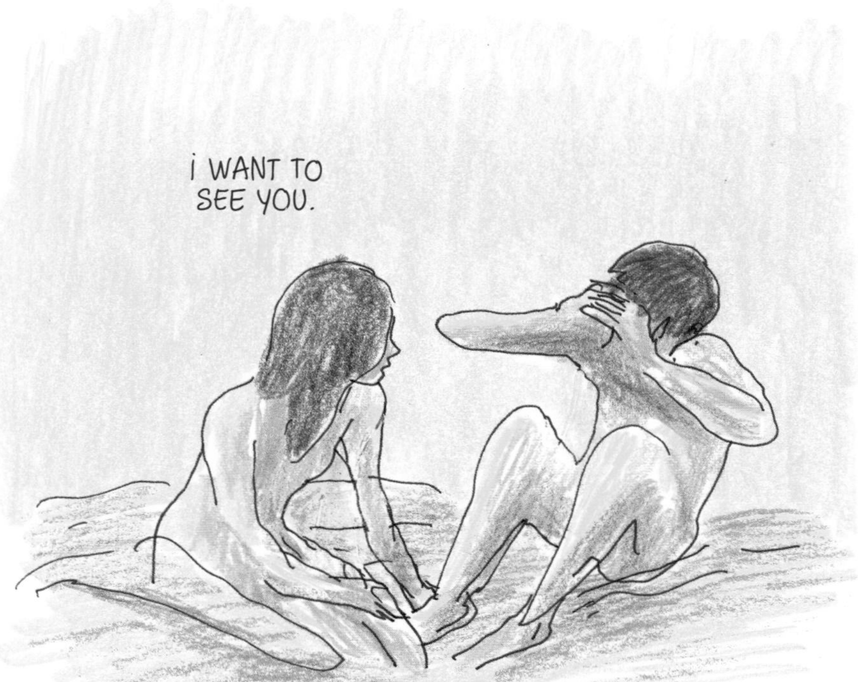
I WANT TO
SEE YOU.

WATCH OUT.
i'M GOING TO HiT YOU
AND iT MiGHT HURT.

GET READY.

WHAM !

AaH...

WHY DID YOU
DO THAT?

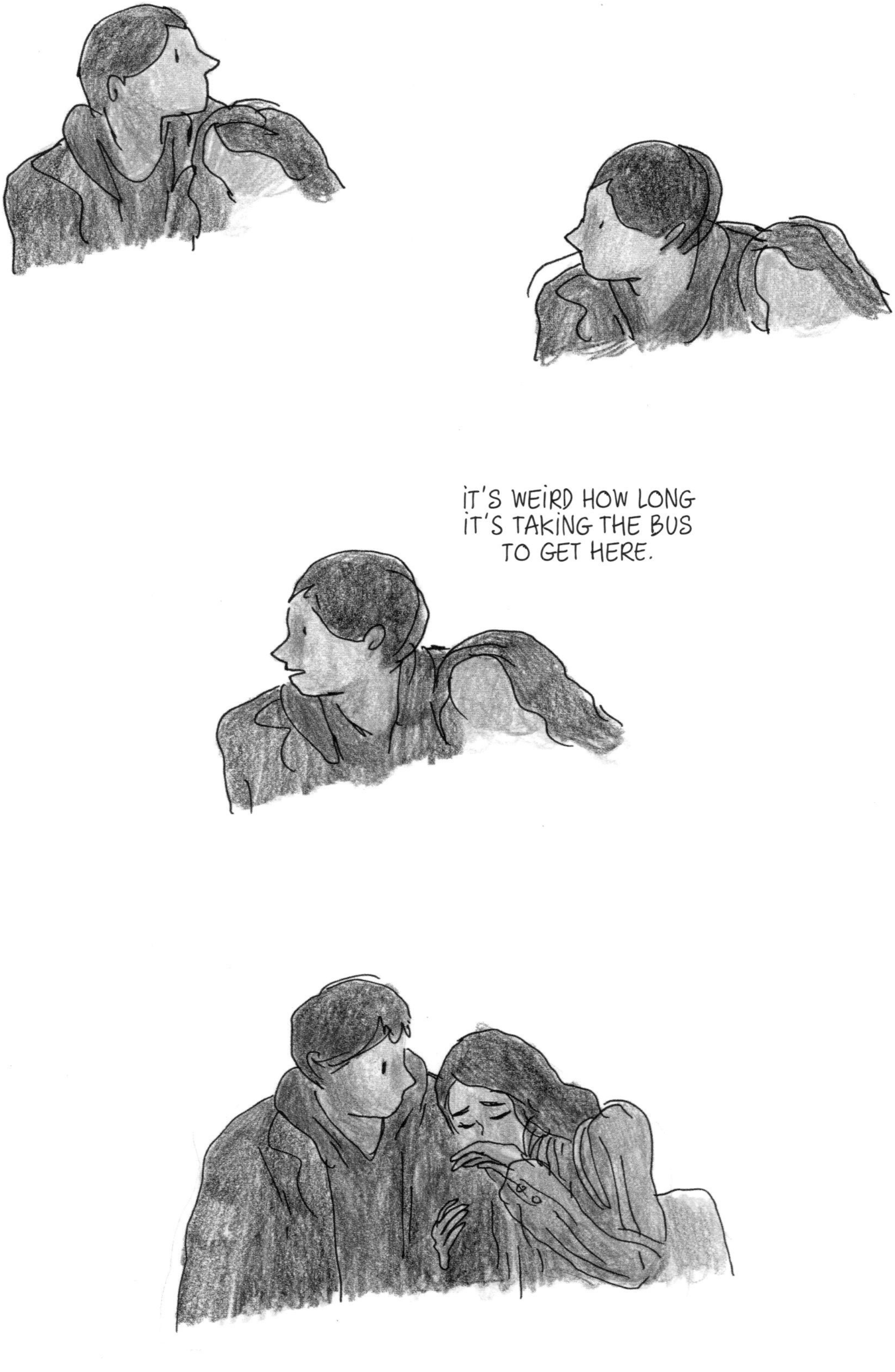
IT'S WEIRD HOW LONG IT'S TAKING THE BUS TO GET HERE.

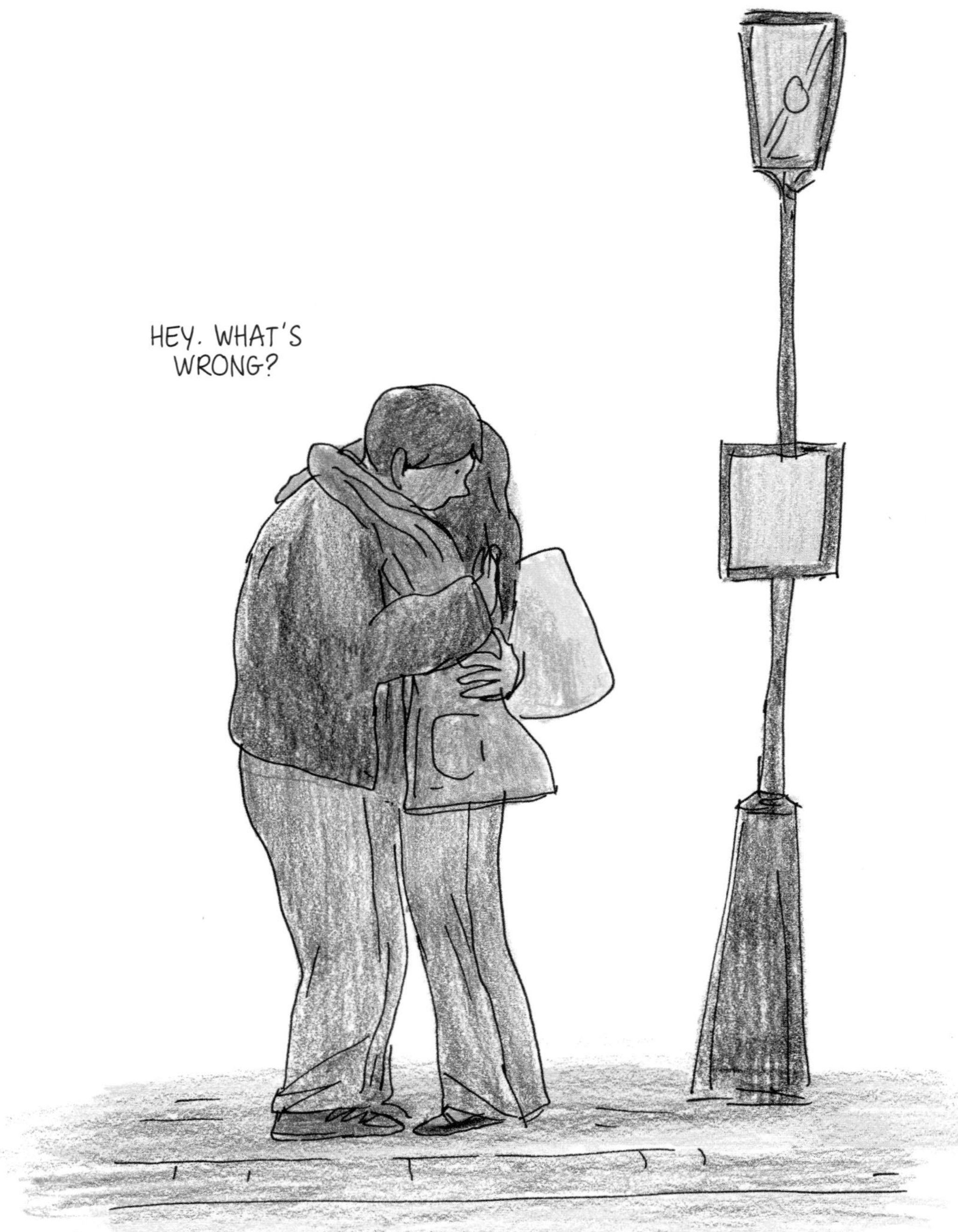
HEY. WHAT'S
WRONG?

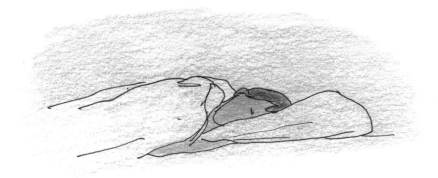

SNif... SNif...

SNNN...

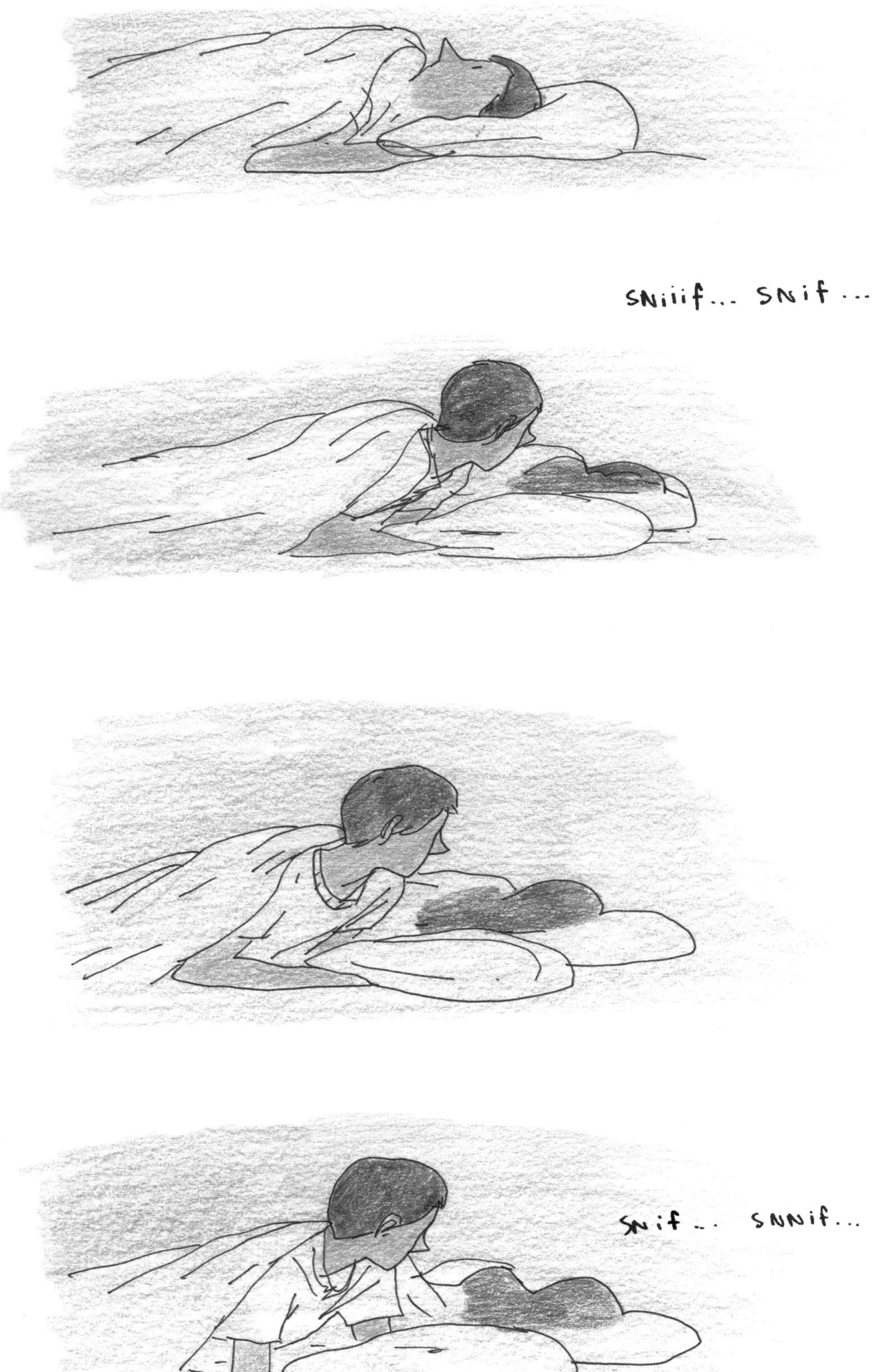
SNiiif... SNif...
SNif... SNNif...

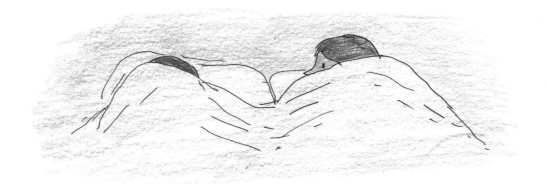

YOU OK?

WHAT'S WRONG?

HHHNNN !

HEY, HEY!
TALK TO ME!

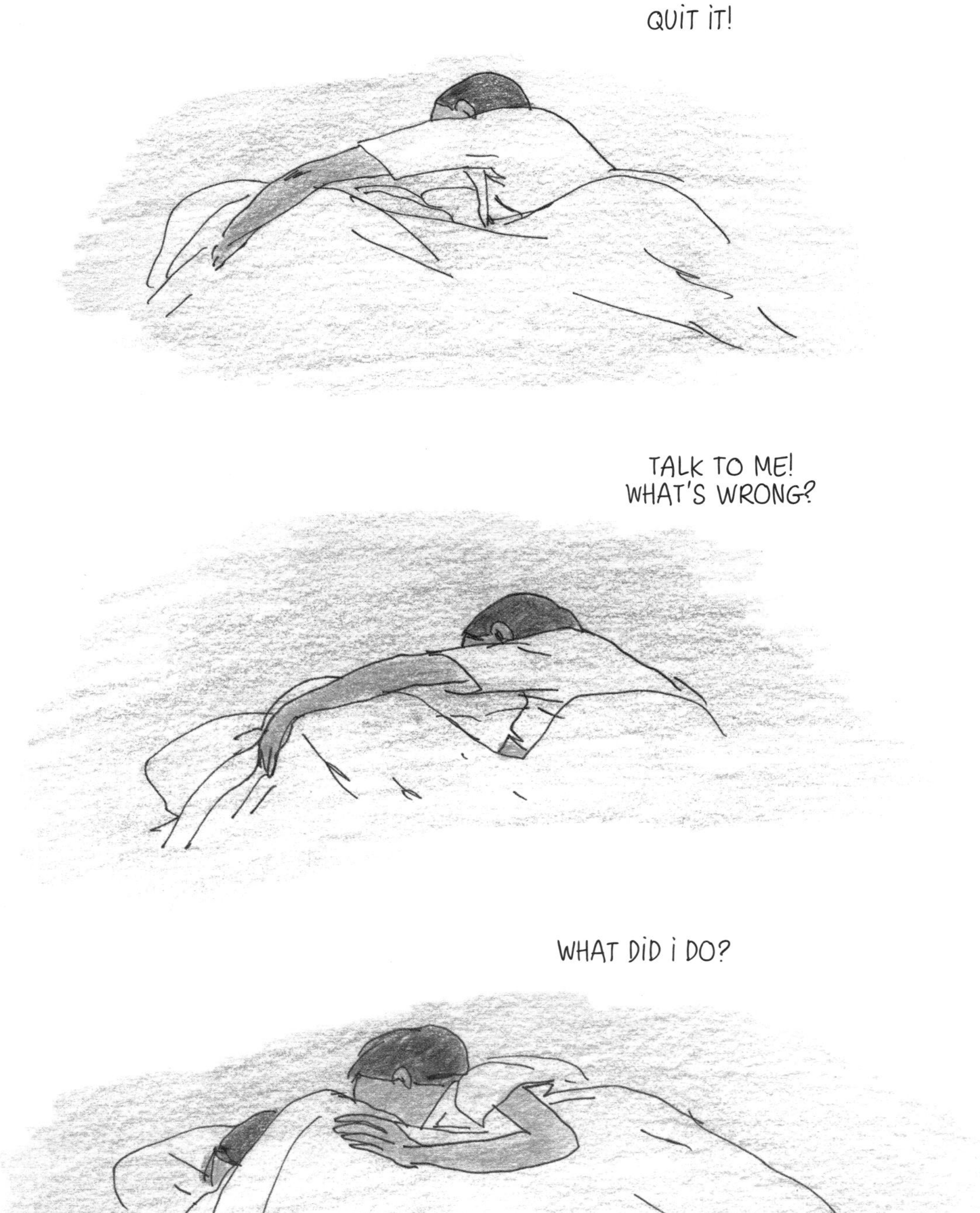
QUIT IT!
TALK TO ME!
WHAT'S WRONG?
WHAT DID I DO?

YOU HURT ME.

STOP!
WHAT DID I DO?
TELL ME!

TELL ME!

QUIT IT!
I'M SORRY!

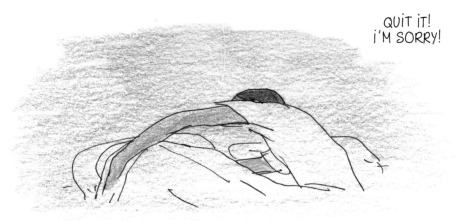

COME ON.
TELL ME
WHAT I DID.

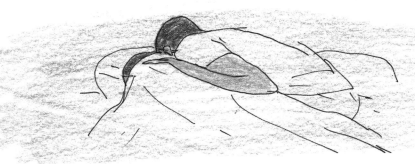

TELL ME...
PLEASE.

WHAT YOU SAID ON
THE PHONE WHEN
YOU HUNG UP.

WHAT, THAT?

YES.

NO. THAT WASN'T
ABOUT YOU. i MEANT
iN GENERAL...
i'M SORRY.

REALLY?

YEAH, i PROMISE.

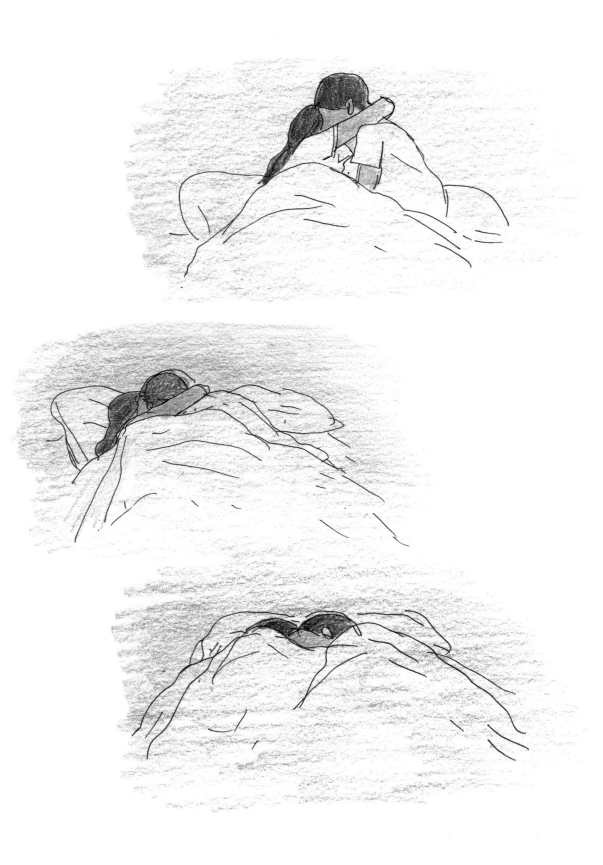

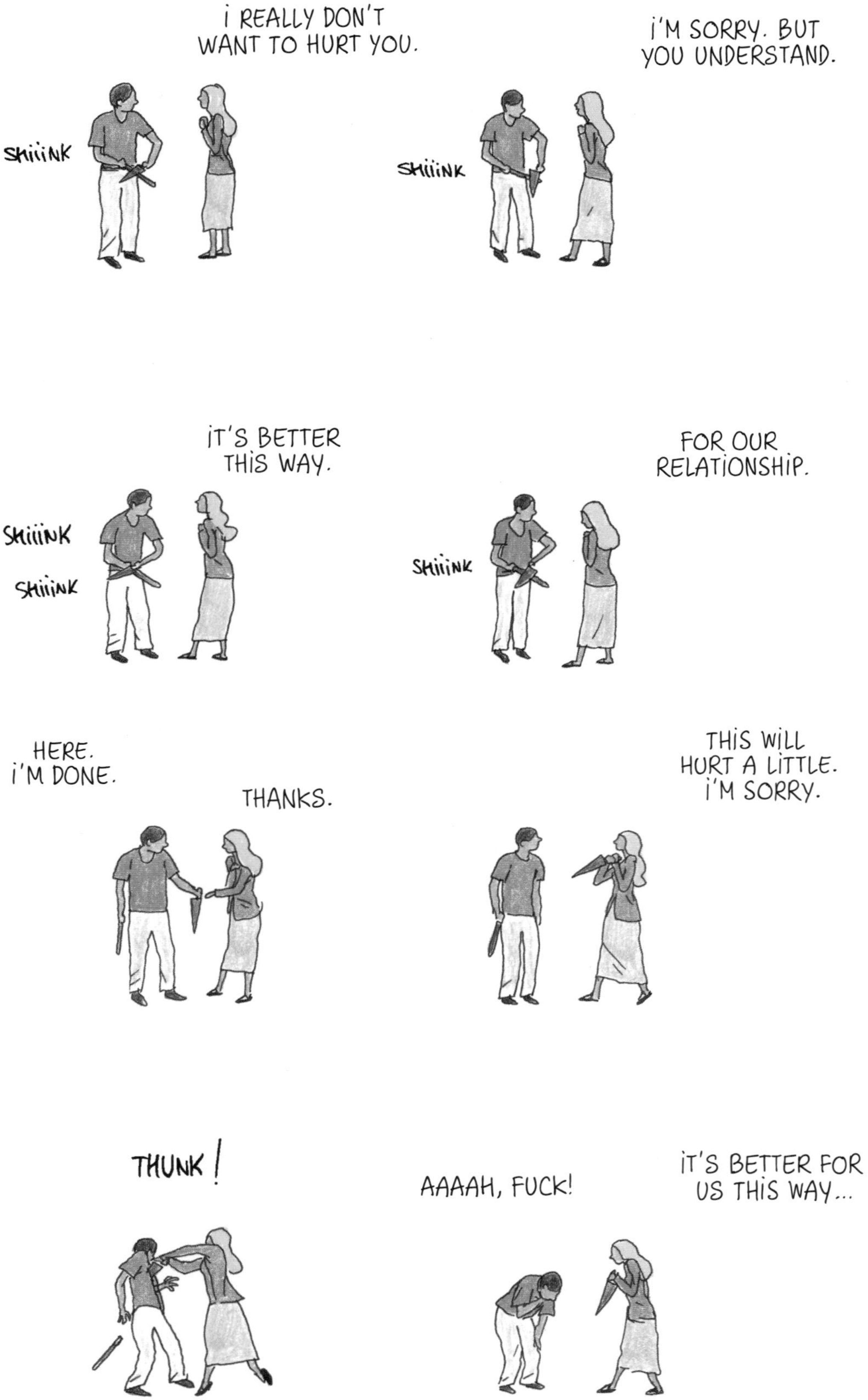
I REALLY DON'T WANT TO HURT YOU.
SHIIINK
I'M SORRY. BUT YOU UNDERSTAND.
SHIIINK
IT'S BETTER THIS WAY.
SHIIINK
SHIIINK
FOR OUR RELATIONSHIP.
SHIIINK
HERE. I'M DONE.
THANKS.
THIS WILL HURT A LITTLE. I'M SORRY.
THUNK!
AAAAH, FUCK!
IT'S BETTER FOR US THIS WAY...

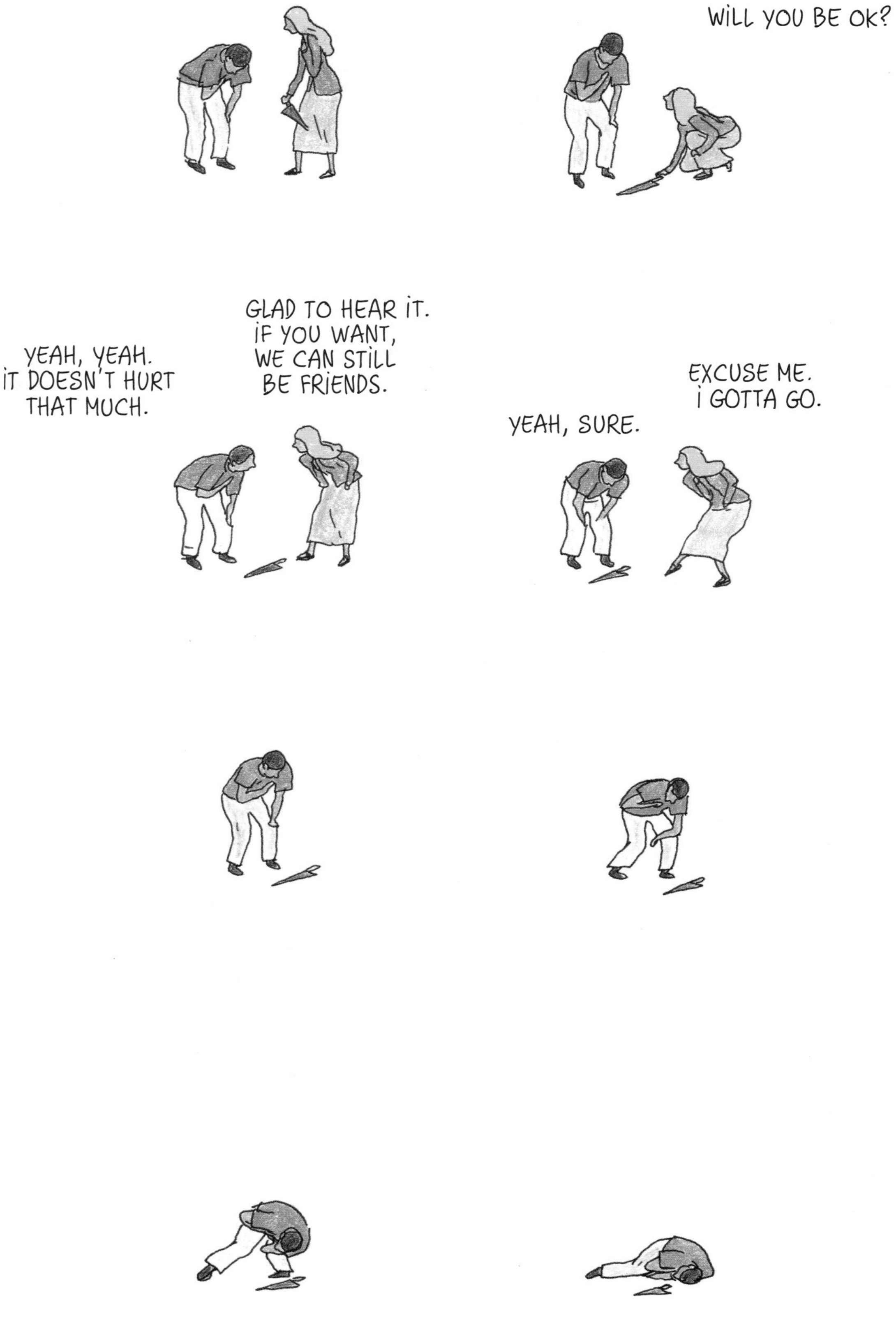
WILL YOU BE OK?
YEAH, YEAH. IT DOESN'T HURT THAT MUCH.
GLAD TO HEAR IT. IF YOU WANT, WE CAN STILL BE FRIENDS.
YEAH, SURE.
EXCUSE ME. I GOTTA GO.

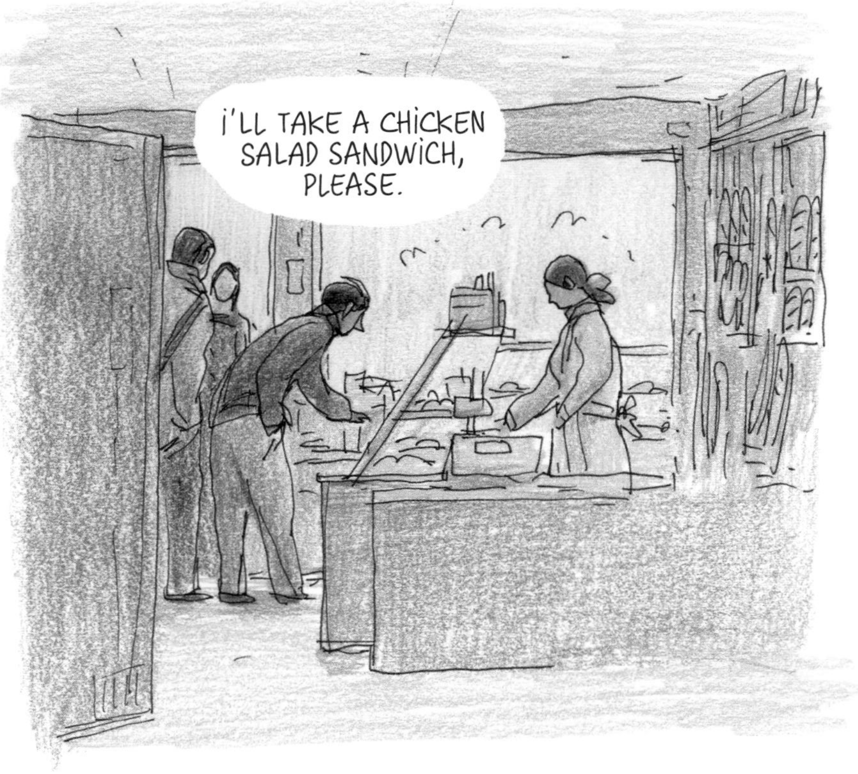
I'LL TAKE A CHICKEN SALAD SANDWICH, PLEASE.

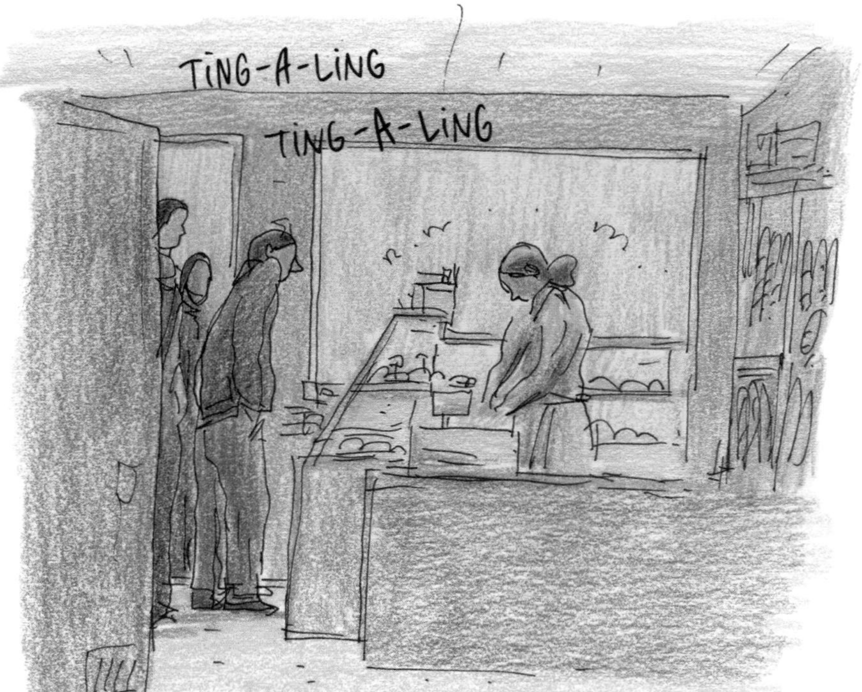
TING-A-LING
TING-A-LING

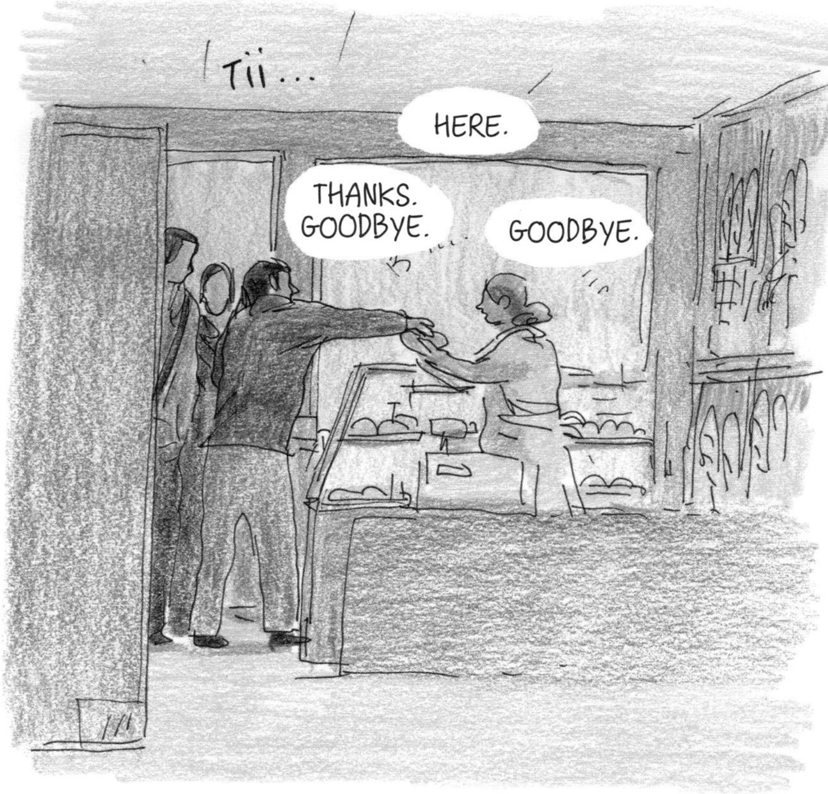
Tii...
HERE.
THANKS. GOODBYE.
GOODBYE.

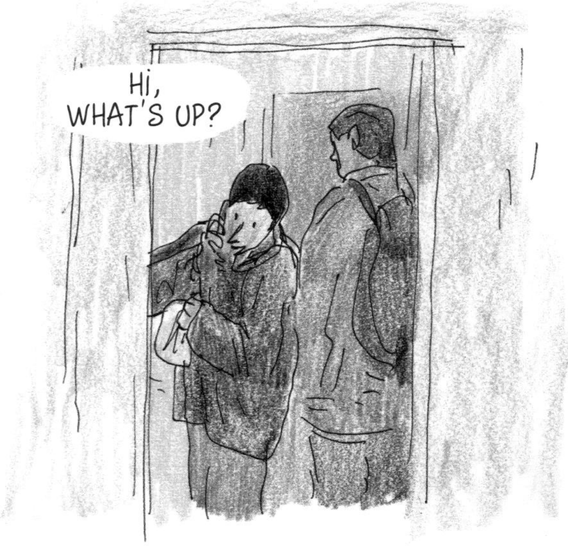
Hi, WHAT'S UP?

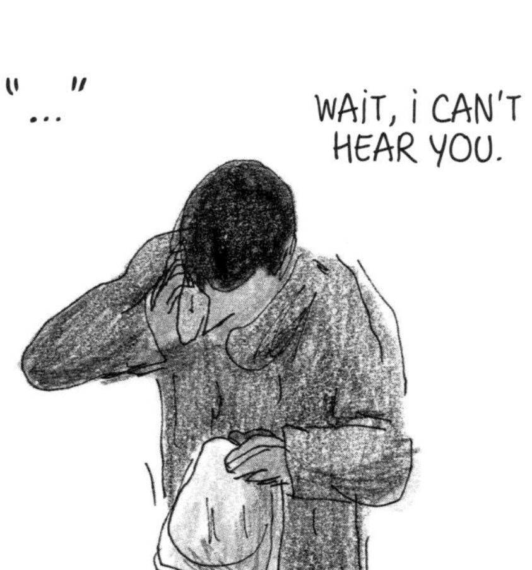
"..."
WAIT, I CAN'T HEAR YOU.

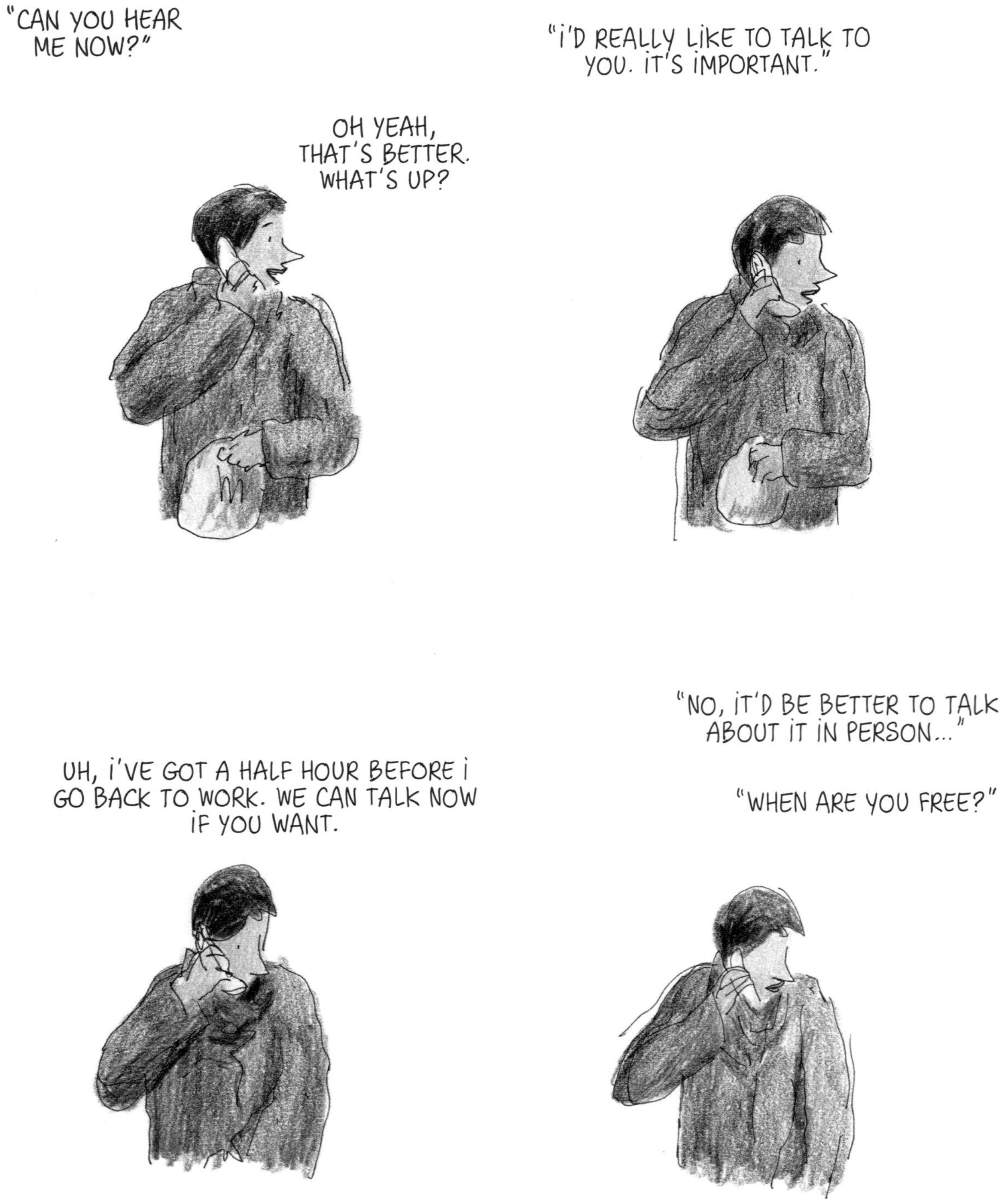
"CAN YOU HEAR ME NOW?"
OH YEAH, THAT'S BETTER. WHAT'S UP?
"I'D REALLY LIKE TO TALK TO YOU. IT'S IMPORTANT."
UH, I'VE GOT A HALF HOUR BEFORE I GO BACK TO WORK. WE CAN TALK NOW IF YOU WANT.
"NO, IT'D BE BETTER TO TALK ABOUT IT IN PERSON..."
"WHEN ARE YOU FREE?"

i DUNNO...

"OR WE CAN
TALK ABOUT IT
ON THE PHONE
NOW."

NO, NO. i'D RATHER DO iT
FACE-TO-FACE.

i'LL CALL YOU WHEN i GET
OFF WORK TONiGHT.

"SEE YOU SOON,
THEN."

YEAH, SEE YOU.

"SOMEDAY YOU'LL UNDERSTAND."
"SOMEDAY YOU'LL UNDERSTAND."
11 TO 14
YOUR SERVE.

"SOMEDAY YOU'LL UNDERSTAND."

WHY? WHAT IS THERE TO UNDERSTAND?

YOU'RE A LIAR. THAT'S ALL THERE IS TO UNDERSTAND.

THAT SEEMS
CLEAR TO ME.

LISTEN, BABE,
i'LL TELL YOU
WHAT THERE iS
TO UNDERSTAND.

iF YOU TAKE A STEP
BACK, YOU'LL SEE
THAT WHAT YOU'RE
SAYiNG...

IT STINKS... LIKE
A PILE OF SHIT.

YEAH, IT'S A
PILE OF SHIT.

ABSOLUTE
BULLSHIT.
I'M TELLING IT
LIKE IT IS.

YOU'LL REALIZE
YOU DON'T KNOW
YOURSELF AT ALL.

AND I'M NOT JUST
SAYING THAT. I
WENT THROUGH IT—

SO DON'T TELL ME I
HAVE TO UNDERSTAND
WHATEVER IT IS.

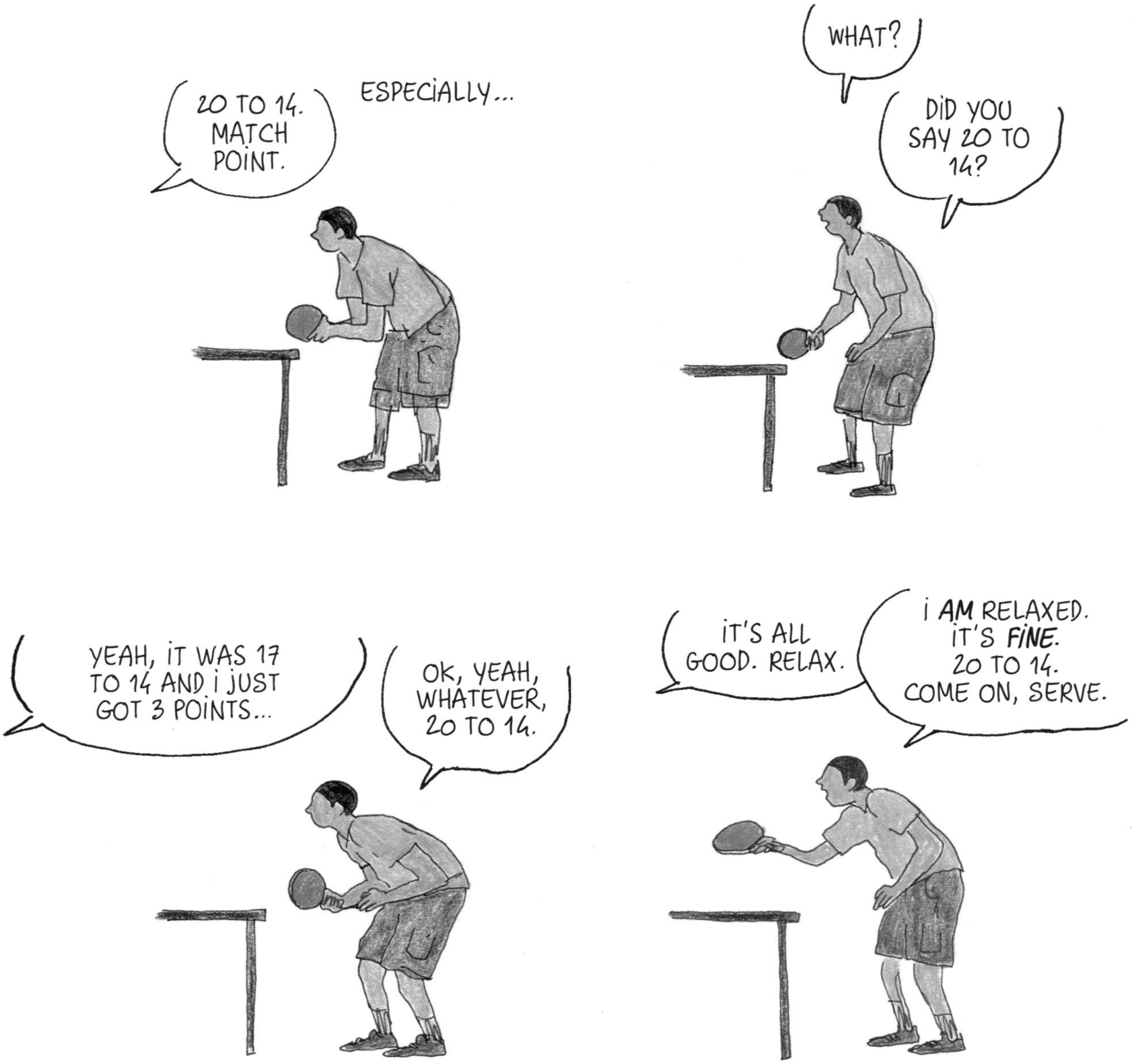
20 TO 14. MATCH POINT.
ESPECIALLY...
WHAT?
DID YOU SAY 20 TO 14?
YEAH, IT WAS 17 TO 14 AND I JUST GOT 3 POINTS...
OK, YEAH, WHATEVER, 20 TO 14.
IT'S ALL GOOD. RELAX.
I **AM** RELAXED. IT'S ***FINE.*** 20 TO 14. COME ON, SERVE.

CLACK !

SHIT!
"SOMEDAY YOU'LL UNDERSTAND."

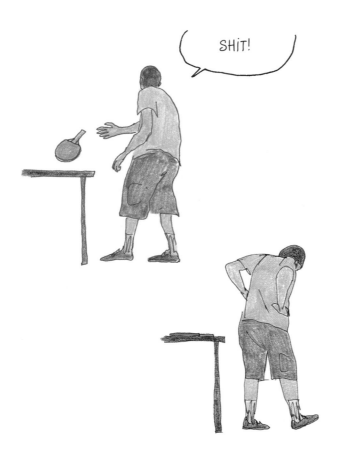

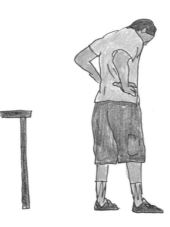

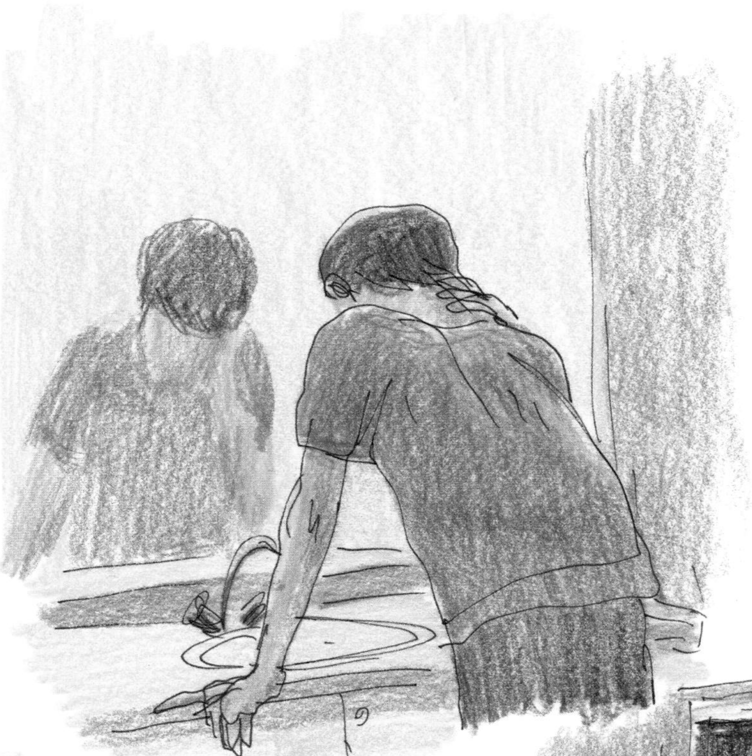

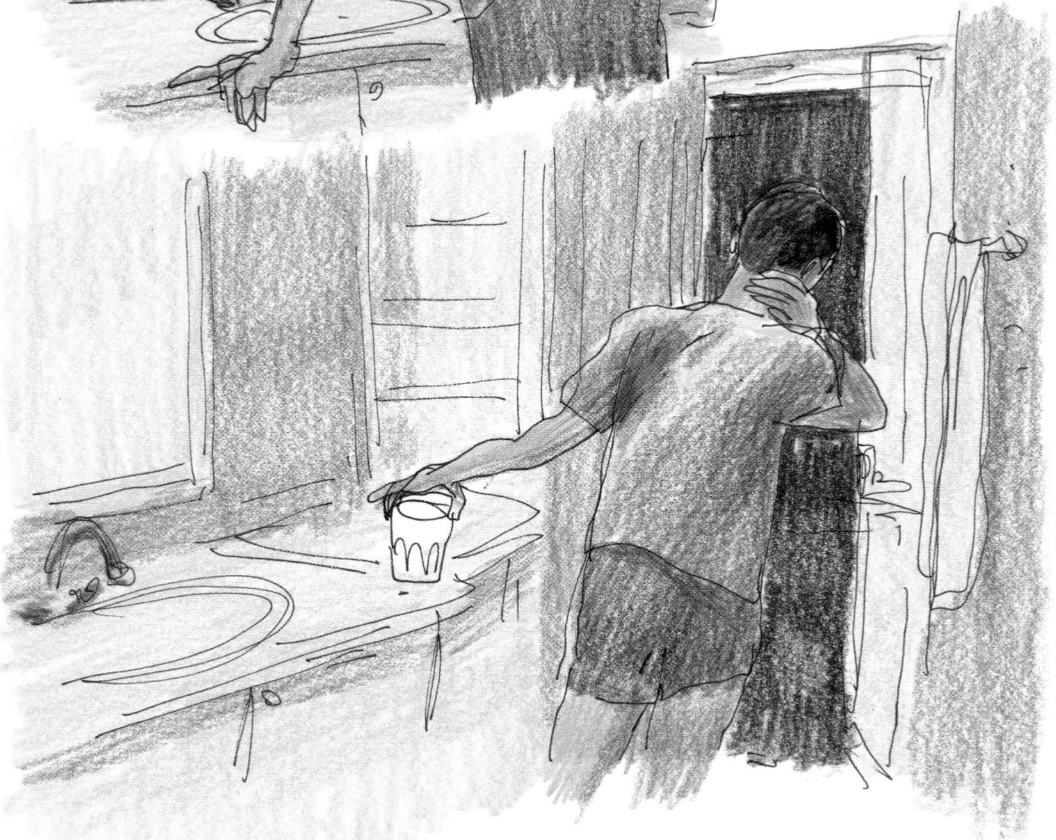

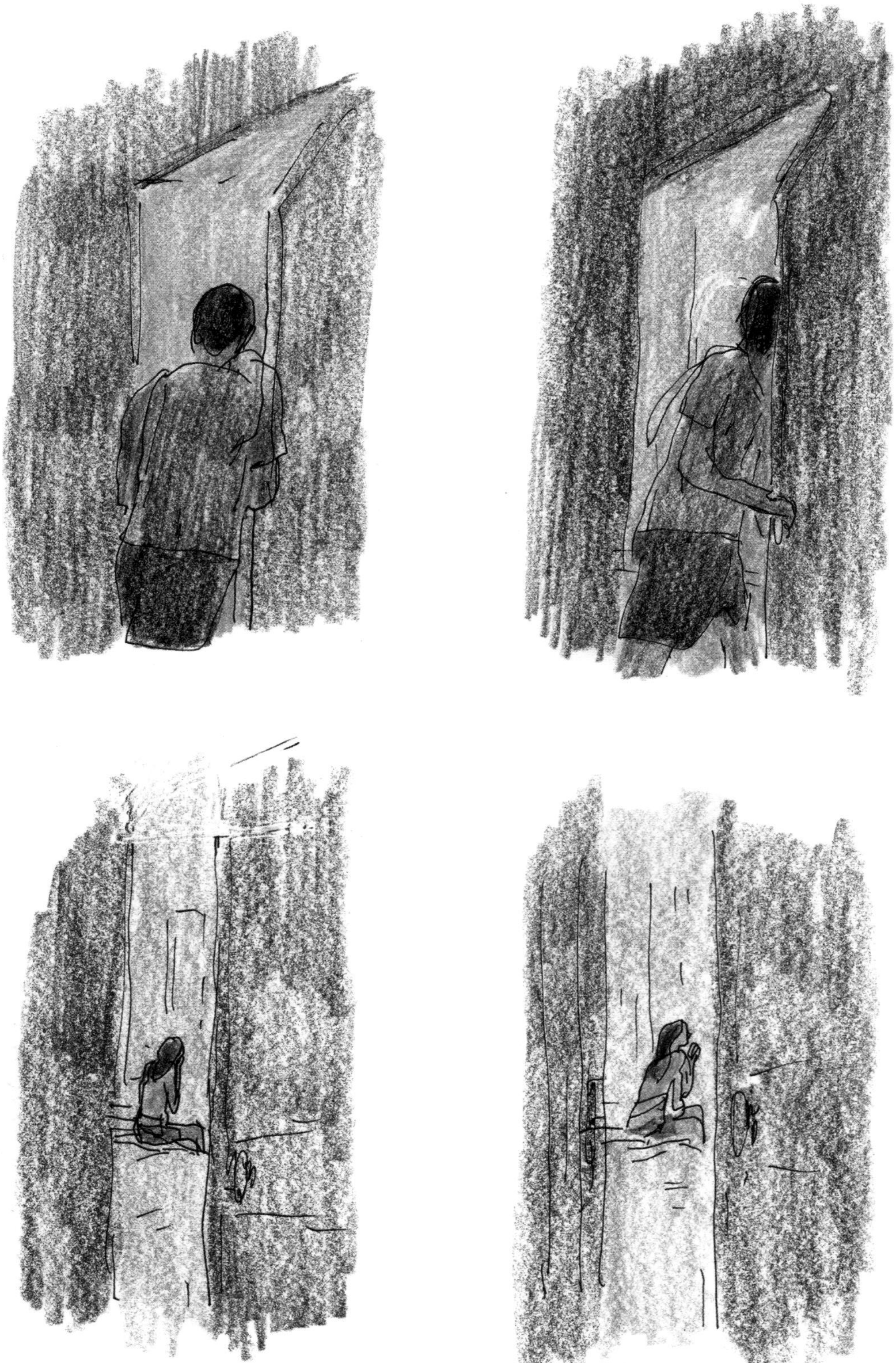

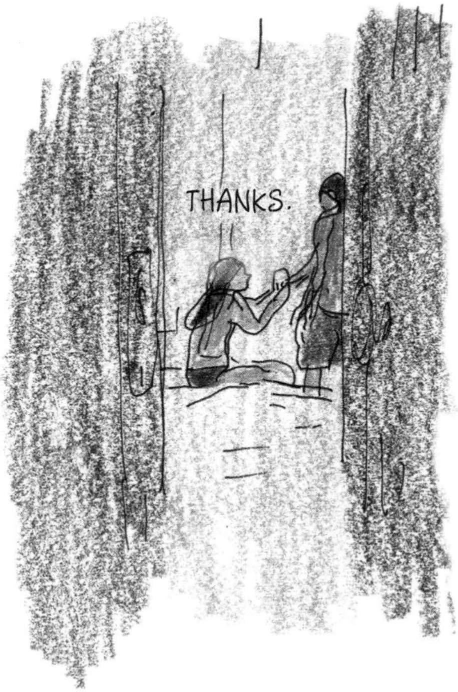
THANKS.

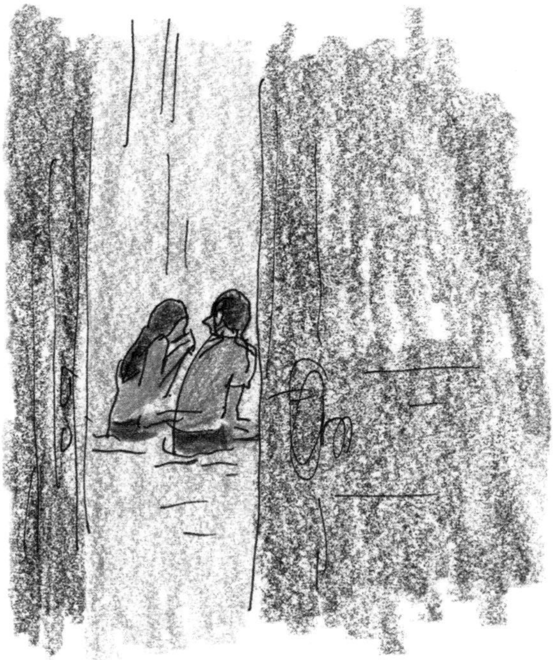

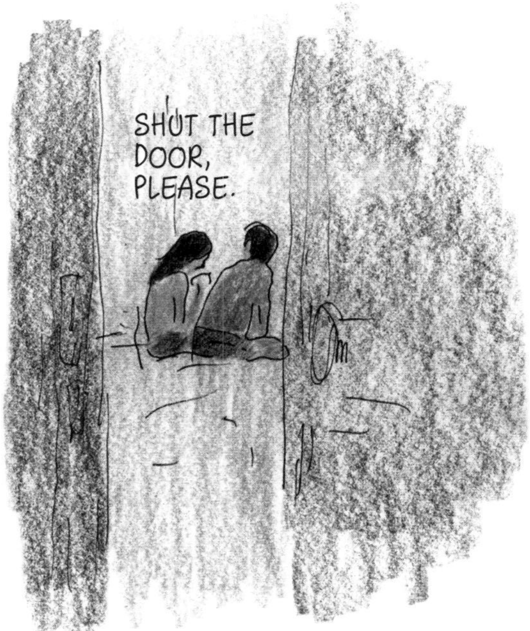
SHUT THE DOOR, PLEASE.

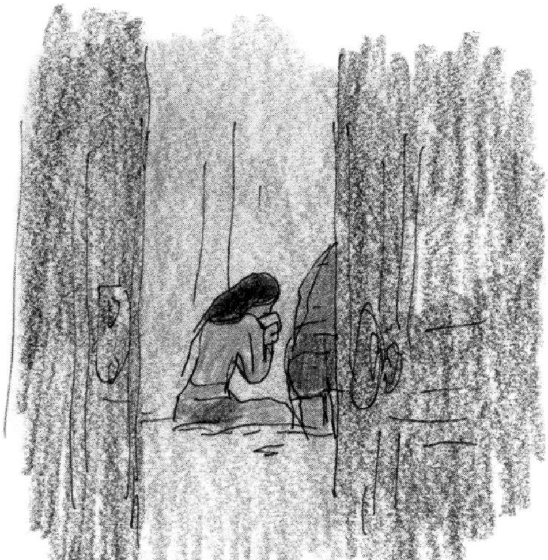

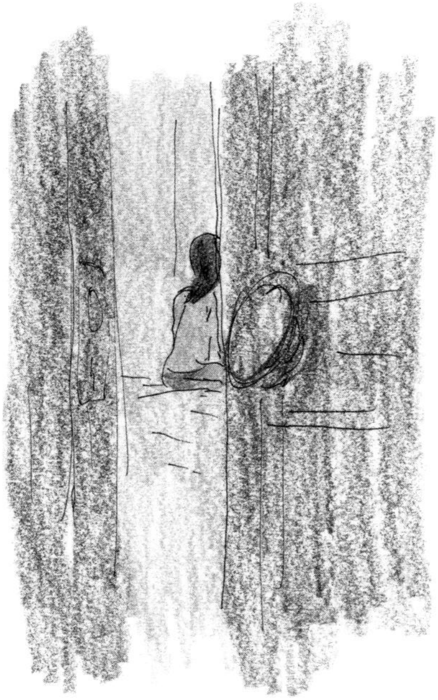

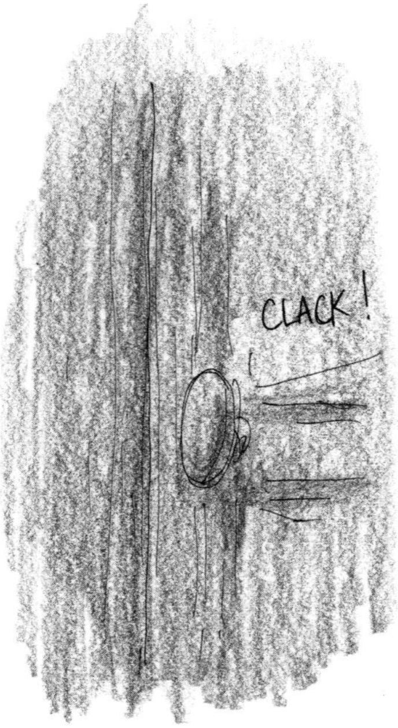
CLACK!

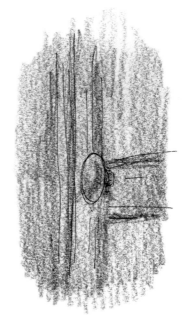

READY TO ORDER?

YES, i'D
LiKE ONE
BREAK-UP,
PLEASE.

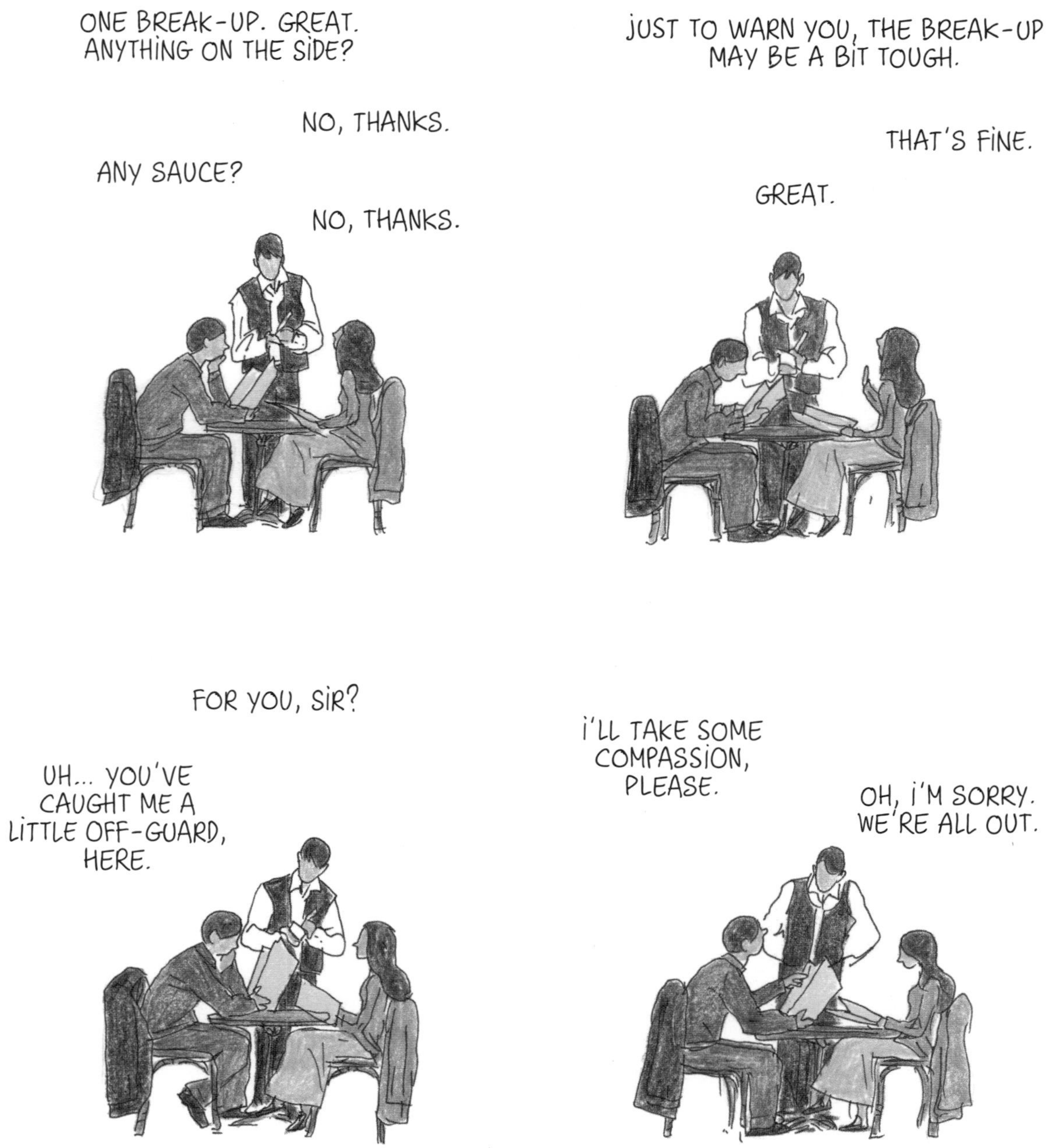
ONE BREAK-UP. GREAT. ANYTHING ON THE SIDE?
NO, THANKS.
ANY SAUCE?
NO, THANKS.
JUST TO WARN YOU, THE BREAK-UP MAY BE A BIT TOUGH.
THAT'S FINE.
GREAT.
FOR YOU, SIR?
UH... YOU'VE CAUGHT ME A LITTLE OFF-GUARD, HERE.
I'LL TAKE SOME COMPASSION, PLEASE.
OH, I'M SORRY. WE'RE ALL OUT.

OH... OK. i SUPPOSE YOU'RE
FRESH OUT OF EMPATHY, TOO.

WE ARE.

UM, WELL, WHAT ABOUT
A LiTTLE TENDERNESS?

i'M SORRY.
THAT'S NOT ON
TODAY'S MENU.

NOT A BiG DEAL.
i'LL JUST HAVE A
DRiNK.

NOTHING TO EAT?
i CAN ASK THE CHEF TO
MAKE YOU SOMETHING.

MAYBE A BiT OF
HOPE, SOMETHING
LIKE THAT?

YEAH, THAT
SOUNDS GOOD.
I'LL HAVE THAT.

PERFECT.

A DRINK
TO GET
STARTED?

NO, NO.
WE'RE FINE,
THANKS.

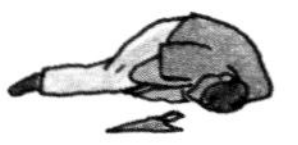

BASTIEN VIVÈS is a Parisian who has drawn or collaborated on more than a dozen graphic novels since his published debut in 2006. The Angoulême International Comics Festival granted Vivès the "Revelation" Award in 2009 and the prize for best series in 2015.

JENNA ALLEN is a freelance translator based in Colorado.

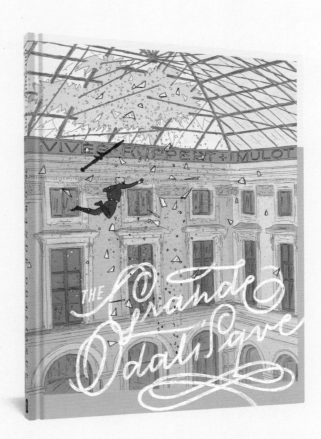

THE GRANDE ODALISQUE

Ruppert & Mulot / Bastien Vivès

978-1-68396-402-5 • $24.99

In this impossibly funny and sexy action-packed thriller, Alex and Carole are childhood friends who have become literal partners in crime. Now they're assembling a crew to pull off their biggest heist yet — stealing the Ingres masterpiece *The Grande Odalisque* from the Louvre.

Look for the sequel to *The Grande Odalisque*, *Olympia*, coming 2022 from Fantagraphics.